THE GIRL GUIDES
ASSOCIATION

OWNIE ANNUAL 1981

Purnell

SBN 361 04674 X
Published 1980 by Purnell Books,
Berkshire House, Queen Street,
Maidenhead, Berkshire
Made and printed in Great Britain by
Purnell & Sons Limited,
Paulton (Bristol) and London

Contents

Make a Brownie Doll 5

Harriet in a Hurry 6
Nancy Bryant

Thinking Day Puzzle 10
P M Stevens

A Prayer 11
S Rothwell

Dear Diary 12

Brownies of the Midnight Sun 15
M Edwards

Puzzle Pie 18

The Brownie Who Forgot 19
N Windridge

Carnivals and Revels 20

Plays and Parties 21

Brownies Make Things 22
N Windridge
P Horton

Guide Camp Puzzle 22
A Brambleby

Brownies Round the World 24

Step into Christmas—Game 26

Random Snapshots—Photographs 28

Poets' Corner 30

Crossword Puzzle 30

What Good is a Brownie? 31
M Coverdale

It's a Challenge 32

Monkey Business 33
A true story

Pony Poems 34

The Silver Horseshoe 36
E Catley

Where Do They Go in Winter? 40

Can You Find the Way? 42

Laugh-In 43

A Good Turn Every Day—Play 44
B Boydell

Brownies Lend a Hand—Puzzles 48

Bells and Badges 49

Express Delivery Service for Seeds 50
D Pilcher

Peeps at Packs—Photographs 52

The Mystery Next Door—Picture Strip 54

Follow the Trail—Game 56

Meet Betsy the Brownie! 58

Brownies Make Things—Photograph 60

Happy Holidays—Photographs 61

Is Your Name Smith? 62

Do You Know These Six Birds? 63

Baffled Birds—Puzzle 63
D Pilcher

Fun Days' Photographs 64

Brownies Help at Home—Puzzles 65

The New Brownie—Story 66
M Aspinall

Orange Appeal!—Things to Make 68

Make Your Own Winter Flowers 69
P Bould

Christmas Around the World 70

Brownie Badge Sewing Cards 72
D Pilcher

Be a Busy Brownie 73

Potato-Cut Printing 74

Answers to the Puzzles 75

Brownies Keep Fit—Puzzles 76

Funny Photos 77

Make a Brownie Doll

It's knitted as a tube, then shaped by stitching. Ask Mummy to lend a hand with it if you get stuck.

Materials Required
Oddments of double knitting wool in dark-brown, brown, white, cream, yellow, gold.
A pair of No.9 knitting needles.
Kapok for stuffing.

Abbreviations
K., knit plain; p., purl; st., stitch; tog., together; s.s., stocking st (knit on the right side and p. on the wrong side); d.b., dark-brown; b., brown; w., white; c., cream; y., yellow; g., gold.
The directions given in the brackets are worked the number of times stated after the last bracket.

The Body
With No.9 needles and d.b., cast on 32 stitches.
The doll is worked entirely in s.s., beginning with a k.row, so only the colour details are given, joining and breaking colours as required.
Work 4 rows in d.b. (shoes).
8 rows in white (socks)
10 rows in brown (uniform)
2 rows in d.b. (belt)
10 rows in brown (uniform)
8 rows in cream (face)
2 rows in yellow (hair)
10 rows in d.b. (hat)
To shape top of head:
1st row: k.3, k.2tog (k.6.,k.2 tog) 3 times, k.3. (28sts).
2nd row: p.3, (p.2 tog., p.5) 3 times p.2tog., p.2. (24sts)
3rd row: k.2, (k.2tog, k.4) 3 times, k.2 tog., k.2.
4th row: p.2 (p.2tog., p.3) 3 times, p.2tog., p.1.

5th row: k.2tog., k3 (k.2 tog., k.2) twice, k.2tog., k.1.
6th row: (p.1,p.2tog) 4 times (8sts)
7th row: (k.2tog) 4 times. (4sts)
8th row: (p.2tog.) twice.
Take remaining 2 sts tog. and fasten off.

To Make Up
Press lightly. Join back seam from top of head to cast-on edge. Stuff firmly, then close opening; stitch up centre of legs to top of socks. Shape arms by stitching 2 cm below neck and 1½ cm in from sides to just below belt. Sew a running stitch round neck and draw tightly to form head shape. Using yellow wool and 9 strands in each, make 2 plaits and attach at side, on hair line. Using b., make bow for each. Finish hat. Cast on 38 sts. Work 2 rows in k.1.p.1. and cast off; sew to hat at top of hair line.

Tie
Cast on 36sts in gold, work 1 row in s.s. Cast off.
Embroider eyes in blue wool, mouth in red. To make pom-pom, wrap d.b. round finger a few times; fasten with needle and wool to hat and then cut.

5

Harriet in a Hurry

"Oh, Harriet!" cried Mrs Larston, the Brownie Guider, as the stand of postcards in the village shop tipped forward and nearly fell. "Do be careful!"

"This shop's too small for Harriet when she's in a hurry," laughed one of the Brownies.

"And she always is!" giggled another.

"There isn't much room in here," said Mrs Larston, kindly, "so it's easy to knock things over."

But Harriet knew that the Brownie Guider was only being kind. She *was* always doing things in a rush. She was always falling about or upsetting things as a result of being in a hurry. Disconsolately, she shuffled out of the shop and stood looking in through the window. The shop was full of fascinating things, from which Harriet and the other Brownies would be able to choose presents to take home when Pack holiday ended.

The trouble with Harriet was that she became so enthusiastic and excited about everything that took her fancy that she didn't stop to think but just charged in, regardless of what might happen from her hurried actions.

"Oh, if only I could be more like Daphne!" she murmured to herself.

Daphne was everything she wasn't. Always neat and tidy, she did everything slowly, carefully and well. Even in a strong wind her short hair never looked out of place, whereas Harriet's usually looked windblown even when there wasn't a wind!

During the Pack holiday, Harriet watched Daphne admiringly and determined to be more like her, but she soon forgot and a few minutes later would be rushing off impulsively without a thought, most likely leaving a trail of damage behind her.

Mrs Larston and the Brownies came out of the shop, and Harriet ran to join them. Eager to walk with Daphne, she leapt

Daphne had bought an ice-cream, most of which now landed in her face

from the kerb without looking, and straight into a muddy puddle. Unable to stop herself, she slid in the mud and ended with a bump against Daphne. Unfortunately, Daphne had bought an ice-cream, most of which now landed in her face.

"I'm sorry, Daphne!" gasped Harriet.

Daphne spluttered. She was annoyed, but she managed to stammer out, "It's—it's all right, Harriet."

"Really, Harriet," said Mrs Larston, hurrying to Daphne's aid with a handkerchief, "you must stop to think! If only you wouldn't do everything in such a hurry these things wouldn't happen."

That afternoon, with Mrs Larston and the Tawny, the Pack set off on a nature-trail in Warren Woods. They hadn't been to the Warren Brownie House before. As they came to a fork in a lane, they saw two youths, evidently from the village, sitting on a stile. The youths looked at them with interest.

"Where are you going?" asked one of them.

Harriet spoke up. "To Warren Woods."

Looking at the Brownies and grinning, the second youth said, "You'd better hurry past the old ruined castle. It's haunted."

"Aye, there's a ghost there all right," agreed his companion, making a hideous face at them.

"Stuff and nonsense!" said Mrs Larston. "Come along, Brownies."

They left the youths grinning. Soon they passed the ruin of the old castle. Sheep and lambs were grazing on the grass around it. The moat surrounding it was well filled with water after the heavy rain of the past few days.

"Oo-er, doesn't it look deep!" cried Sandra, the Elf Sixer, gazing into the moat.

"The ruin looks as if it could be haunted," remarked her Second, Fiona.

"There are no such things as ghosts or haunted ruins," Mrs Larston told them, "so don't go getting ideas into your heads and frightening each other."

The old ruin did look dark and forlorn, although part of the roof still remained. Even so, the Brownies would have risked going into it if they could have cuddled the newly born lambs that followed their mother sheep through the ruins.

Warren Woods were green and beautiful. The Brownies began to follow the nature-trail, and collected grasses, leaves and bark for the Pack nature-book they were making. A grey squirrel leapt from a branch of an oak-tree near which Harriet was standing, and Harriet stayed to follow its movements.

"Come on, Harriet!" called Mrs Larston.

As usual, not stopping to see

Mrs Larston examined her ankle. "It's not a break, but a sprain," she pronounced

where she was going, Harriet hurtled off, scattering wet mud in all directions.

Daphne hastily tried to get out of her way, tripped over an exposed tree-root, and fell.

"Oh!" she cried. Her face turned white. She tried to stand, but sat quickly down again, clutching her ankle.

Mrs Larston examined her ankle. "It's not a break, but a sprain," she pronounced. "We'll help Daphne back to the track outside the woods; then she can sit on the grass while I go back to the Brownie House and fetch my car. Tawny will look after you till I get back."

With Tawny holding one arm, and Brownies taking it in turns to help on the other side, Daphne managed to reach the track outside the woods. Several of the Brownies elected to go back to

the Brownie House with the Guider, while a few remained behind with Tawny and Daphne.

"It's quite a long walk back to the Brownie House," said Mrs Larston, "but you'll be able to amuse yourselves until I get back with the car."

"I'll look after her," Harriet declared.

Mrs Larston looked rather wryly at her, but said nothing as she and the Brownies hurried off in the direction of the Brownie House.

"It was all my fault," Harriet admitted to Daphne.

"I can't think why you always do everything in a hurry, Harriet," said Daphne. "I don't rush about like you."

"I know. I wish I could be more like you," said Harriet. "Oh, dear, it's beginning to rain!"

"We'd better shelter in the woods," said Sandra, one of the Brownies who had stayed.

"We'll soon get soaked under the trees," Mandy, the Sprite

Sixer, said. "It's coming down heavily."

"We'd better go into the ruin," said Tawny. "We'll keep dry there."

"Oh, no, I couldn't!" cried Sandra.

"I'd rather get wet than go in there," said Amy Dodds, one of the Kelpies.

The rain was becoming heavy. While Tawny was persuading some of the Brownies that there was nothing to fear, Harriet grabbed Daphne's arm. "Come on! You're getting wet. I'll help you into the ruin. I'm not scared. We'll be wet through in no time under these trees; they're dripping rain already."

It was true. The trees, although thick, were so soaked with the heavy rain that had come down during the week that they provided poor shelter. Catherine, Joanna and Hilary joined Harriet in helping Daphne into the ruined castle, where she found a smooth piece of stonework to sit on under the part of the roof that remained intact.

"We'll be drier here than we would be under the trees," remarked Catherine. "Oh, the others are coming with Tawny now. I don't suppose Brown Owl will be long."

"Unless she has to shelter from the rain herself," said Joanna. "She hasn't got a—oh, what's that?"

A strange sound had come from somewhere behind them. Glancing fearfully round, the Brownies saw a grey shape move behind one of the ruined walls. With their thoughts racing back to what the village youths had told them about the old castle being haunted, the Brownies froze. Then Daphne saw the grey shape move again and jumped

up. Landing on her injured ankle, she let out a loud yell.

This startled not only the Brownies but the grey shape, which Harriet quickly saw was a sheep grazing on the grass among the stonework. The sheep, scared by the sudden movement and noise, plunged away. Then Harriet gave a cry of alarm. Beside the sheep was one of its lambs, not more than a few weeks old. Both sheep and lamb had been grazing at the top of the grassy embankment that sloped steeply down to the moat. As the sheep turned away, the lamb, still shaky on its legs, tumbled over and then went rolling down the steep embankment and into the moat.

As usual, Harriet didn't stop to think. She raced across the

"You poor thing!" she said, cuddling its wet, bedraggled body to her. "I don't think you've come to any harm, though"

grassy patch under the roof of the ruin and almost headlong down the embankment. She was only just in time to catch the lamb as, half submerged, it drifted helplessly out into the moat. Harriet, half in the moat herself, managed to get hold of the little creature and lift it out.

"You poor thing!" she said, cuddling its wet, bedraggled body to her. "I don't think you've come to any harm, though."

The mother sheep stood at the top of the embankment, bleating pathetically.

"Here you are," said Harriet, placing the lamb gently on the grass after climbing back up the embankment. "You take your baby to a safer spot."

The lamb, already recovering from its ducking, bleated in a tiny voice and ran back to its mother, who bleated loudly which Harriet supposed was either a thank you to her for rescuing it or a scolding to the lamb for falling in the moat; she didn't know which.

"I know which it ought to be, anyhow," said Daphne, as Harriet rejoined the Brownies. "You were quick and brave to do what you did, Harriet."

"Well done, Harriet!" cried Tawny.

"She was Harriet in a hurry all right," laughed Catherine.

"A good thing she was too," said Hilary. "It would have been awful if that dear little lamb had drowned."

"You're wet, Harriet," Joanna pointed out.

'I'm not as wet as some of you are!" laughed Harriet.

The Brownies who had lingered in the woods did look rather wet and bedraggled.

"I wish we'd come with you," said Sandra. "You've kept drier than we have—except Harriet."

Daphne told them of Harriet's speed and bravery in rescuing the lamb, and Fiona remarked, "Harriet has done some good by being in a hurry!"

"Brown Owl will be pleased when she hears about it," said Tawny.

Brown Owl was pleased. She arrived in her car soon after this, and took Daphne and Tawny and the wet Brownies back to the Brownie House.

"I shall tell the farmer who owns the sheep that you rescued one of his lambs," she told Harriet. "I know he'll be grateful."

The farmer was very grateful when he heard, and sent along milk, fresh butter and eggs to the Brownie House every day during the Pack's stay there.

Daphne's ankle soon mended, and it didn't stop her from enjoying the Pack holiday, which Harriet decided was the most enjoyable holiday she'd ever had, especially as she became fast friends with Daphne.

"Between now and next Pack holiday," she confided to Daphne, "I shall try to learn not to be in such a hurry."

"I'm not sure you should bother," said Daphne. "You've proved that being in a hurry is sometimes a jolly good thing, especially if you're brave with it as well."

The 4th Bicester Brownie Pack celebrate Thinking Day by dressing in the costumes of countries in many parts of the world and light Thinking Day candles

E D Jones

Thinking Day Puzzle

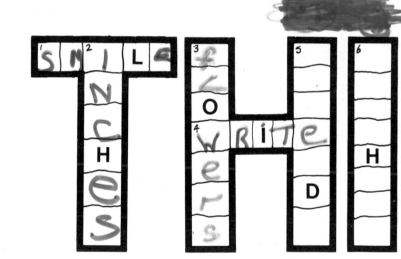

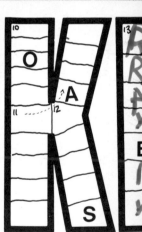

A means Across; **D** means Down

1A—Seen on a Brownie's face (5)

2D—Knitting is still measured in these (6)

3D—Give these fresh water (7)

4A—Put pen to paper (5)

5D—Brownies are this with everyone (7)

6D—What you celebrate on Thinking Day (8)

7D—The Brownie Ring is about this shape (5)

8D—This bird is the emblem of a Guide Patrol (5)

9D—Every day a Brownie does a good one of this (4)

10D—To use night and morning (10)

11A—A bird sits on this (6)

12D—Be careful when you cross these (5)

13D—Brownies say these each day (7)

Please bow your heads and say a prayer
For all in our Movement everywhere,
For young and old, for sick or poor,
That today they may be sure—
WE THINK OF THEM.

For those who suffer famine and floods
And fire that destroys their worldly goods,
We ask relief from fear and pain
That their spirits may rise again,
And so today they may be sure
WE THINK OF THEM.

Lift up your hearts to the coming year;
Spring and summer will soon be here.
Lend a Hand and do your best,
Strive to succeed whatever the test.
Lift up your hearts to God this day,
Bless our Founders on this their day,
That today they may be sure—
WE THINK OF THEM.

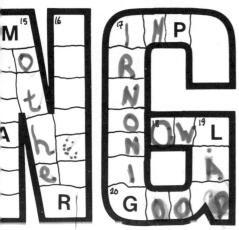

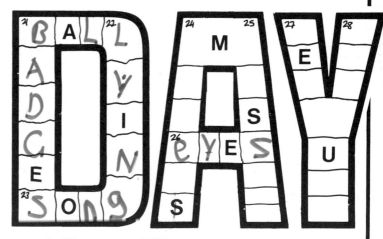

14D—The princess who is President of the Girl Guides Association (8)

15D—You are her daughter (6)

16D—Someone to L.A.H. to at school (7)

17A—Mischievous Brownies in a Six (4)

17D—You may be doing this with clothes (7)

18A—Brown . . .? (3)

19D—You couldn't be a Brownie if you were this (3)

20A—A Brownie always tries to be this (4)

21D—Brownies work for these (6)

21A—You play with this (4)

22D—When in bed you are doing this (5)

23A—You sing this (4)

24D—You may make these for one of your Challenges (6)

25D—Brownies learn to carry this on the Brownie Road (7)

26A—Keep these wide open (4)

27D—Not right (4)

28D—The Pack do this together (7)

Pack Holiday Pleasures

Friday

Mummy thinks I'm in bed asleep by now, but I'm so excited I don't think I'll be able to sleep all night. I've been waiting to go on a Pack Holiday for so long—over a year, really, because of having measles last year and not being able to go. Now it's actually the night before we go, and I just can't believe it's happening at last! My suitcase is all packed and ready for tomorrow morning—well, *almost* ready. I've still to slip *you* in, Diary—and Ted, of course. I hope Sally is taking her teddy bear too—I'll feel so silly if I'm the only person to take her teddy on Pack Holiday with her, but I just *can't* leave him behind—I'll pop him under my pillow as soon as we get there, and maybe no one will notice him.

Saturday

I was up at eight o'clock today to be ready for the coach leaving at 9—I felt a bit sad saying goodbye to Mummy and Daddy, but at least I didn't *cry*, like Mandy Ellis. What a baby! We all chose our seats in the coach and Brown Owl soon had us singing our favourite songs, which even cheered Mandy up. We stopped at a lovely park, where we ate our packed lunches and played on the swings, then we all piled back on the bus. We couldn't wait to arrive at Menzies House! Brown Owl had told us that it used to be the home of a very grand family, before they went to live abroad. When we arrived we all tumbled out of the coach in a rush. The house is very big and full of interesting places to explore. There are even separate servants' quarters, which are now the Pack Holiday "headquarters". It was great

fun choosing our bunk beds—I have an "upstairs" one. I noticed that there were lots of teddy bears on the beds, so I brought Ted out from under the pillow! After tea, we were all very tired, so we went off to get ready for bed early.

Sunday

We had a lovely day today. In the morning we went to the Church service in the village. Lots of the village people said how smart we looked in our uniforms. (They don't have a Brownie Pack here, as it is only a very small village.) We met some of the local children and Brown Owl said we could invite them to a picnic later in the week if the weather was good.

In the afternoon we went for a long

"If that owl joins in, why shouldn't I?" thinks the dog as he joins in the daily Pow-wow on Pack Holiday

Nature walk and found lots of things to collect—wild flowers, pretty stones, grasses and feathers. We played guessing games naming the birds and insects we saw—we even saw a little grey squirrel, but it must have been very shy as it ran away when Brown Owl threw some nuts. Maybe it'll come back for them later.

Monday

We all changed our names today! We are to be "Woodland Creatures" for the

week, so Brown Owl became Foxy, Tawny Owl is now Squirrel, and Tina, our Cook, is Badger. Foxy divided us into three groups for the week—Ladybirds, Bumblebees and Butterflies (I'm a Bumblebee). And just for fun, Tina is going to write out a special menu for us all week with woodland names for the food. Today we had Badger Stew and Hedgehog Pudding. The groups have to make up their own challenges—today the Bumblebees cleaned all the windows of the staff quarters. (I'm glad we didn't have to clean the windows of the *whole* house!) In the afternoon we

Making pastry for the Cook badge on Pack Holiday

went into Littlesham—the village—and bought postcards to send home. It seems a long time since we left.

Tuesday

It was raining when we woke up today and Mandy was sitting on the floor crying because she had fallen out of bed! *And* she's in a bottom bunk! Honestly, she cries about *everything*. In the morning we washed our socks and hung them in a long line over the bath to dry. In the afternoon Squirrel showed us how to make little animals and people from the things we'd collected on our

walk on Sunday. She had a big bag full of things like pipe cleaners and glue to help us. We got into an awful sticky mess, but we were wearing our Brownie aprons, so it didn't matter! I made a sheep by sticking cotton wool all over a bobbin, and making legs from pipe cleaners. After supper we had a pyjama parade, and Squirrel took some photographs of us, to stick into the big scrapbook she is making about our holiday.

Two of the House Orderly Six get busy sweeping up the crumbs after breakfast

W J Beer

Wednesday

The sun was shining again this morning, so we played on the swings near the house until "Smiley", our driver, drove the coach up the drive and we all set off for the shops. It was lovely choosing presents to take home—I bought a teapot stand with a picture on it for Mummy and Daddy, but I'm going to take home the things I made too, because they always say they like "home-made" presents best. We had lunch in a restaurant and then we spent a lot of time having our photographs taken in a "booth"—everyone queued up and at first Foxy was a bit annoyed, but then she joined the queue too and had *her* photographs taken! They looked very funny as she had been making faces at the camera. When we got back to Menzies House in the evening we helped to make little cakes. We had them for supper with our cocoa—Mandy Ellis dropped hers on the floor!

Making toys is one of the popular activities enjoyed on Pack Holiday

Thursday

It was hot and sunny again today, so Foxy said we could have our Teddy Bears' Picnic after all, *and* invite some children from the village. We helped Squirrel and Badger to make little sandwiches and a special orange drink made with honey, which Foxy said Teddy Bears were *very* fond of! There was to be a prize for the best dressed Teddy, so after lunch we all rushed off and raided Squirrel's big bag again. I wrapped my facecloth round Ted and made him a shower cap from a little piece of plastic, and a cardboard toothbrush. Sue's Teddy won first prize—she dressed him up as Santa Claus! In the evening we sang songs round the campfire and Foxy told us about Guides. I can't wait to be eleven and join Guides!

Friday

We didn't know what we were going to do this morning, but Squirrel told us to get ready to go off in the coach after breakfast—on a surprise journey! We all

tried to guess where we were going—I thought maybe we were going back into the town again, but we drove straight through the town and after a while the coach turned into a Safari Park! We saw lions, tigers, buffaloes and giraffes—we had to keep all the windows of the coach closed and it was very exciting when the chimpanzees jumped onto the bonnet of the coach and made funny faces at Smiley! They were ever so funny! We got off the coach at the Lodge by the gate and bought some postcards of the animals. When we were having tea at the open-air restaurant some chimps came up to join us, so we had a chimpanzees' tea party! When we got back Badger had decorated the kitchen and it looked just like a witch's cave—very dark and spooky. She had even put green light bulbs in especially! Squirrel told us all to go off and put on our pyjamas, with the blankets over the top like capes. Then we had a party and Squirrel, Foxy and Badger dressed up and sang songs and did magic tricks for us. We had a great time until we had to go to bed.

Saturday

I'm writing this at home again in my own little bedroom—it seems funny to be in a room all by myself again after being with so many Brownies for a week! It was nice to come back home again, even though it was sad to leave everything behind. Mandy Ellis cried again! But I can't wait till I go up to Guides next year and go to CAMP!

Brownies of the Midnight Sun

North

Scalloway Lerwick

Shetland

0   5   10

I t would puzzle Guides to build a bivouac or any wooden shelter on Shetland. Can you guess why? There isn't any wood! In Shetland, woodland and forest don't exist.

Brownies do, though! You can see some of them in the photographs on the next two pages. Bringing Brownies together here is not easy, for, apart from the county capital, Lerwick, and the old capital of Scalloway, there are no towns. The crofts in which most of the old Shetlanders live are widely scattered along lonely hillsides. This makes attendance at Pack meetings difficult for many girls at all times, and in summer most of them help to get the crops in before bad weather comes.

All the same, the 1st Sandwick Pack meet, work for badges, enjoy themselves, Lend a Hand, and do everthing that town or city Brownies do with enthusiasm and zest.

Where is Shetland? If you take a look at the map of Britain and look right at the top you will see two groups of islands no more than tiny spots on the map. The first group are the Orkney Islands and the second and farthest group are the Shetland Islands.

In the summer, you can easily visit the island by boat from Aberdeen, on the east coast of Scotland's mainland, or you can fly from most big airports; but in winter it is a wild and windy place. The little fishing-boats are often dashed to pieces on the rocks if they are not moored properly. Surprisingly, though, it very rarely snows in Shetland. This is due to a warm wedge of water entering the Atlantic called the Gulf Stream.

In Shetland it is usually windy. This is because the islands are surrounded by water. On the west coast the fierce waters of the Atlantic Ocean crash onto the land, while in the east is the North Sea.

There are approximately a hundred islands, some no more than jagged lumps of rock sticking out of the sea; many provid-

ing safe nesting sites for the hundreds of sea-birds that flock there. From the southern tip of Shetland to the northern point is over 70 miles (43 km).

Much of the land is wild, heather-covered moorland. There are rocky coves, with interesting caves to explore and long sandy beaches, all surrounded by a clear blue sea. There are hundreds of lochs — some so tiny they could fit into your garden. They are full of fine brown trout — very tasty!

Most of the fish that find their way into the fishermongers' shops of England comes from the rich Shetland waters. In the harbour, fishing-boats from many different parts of Europe can be seen, all attracted to Shetland for its fish. In Shetland there are more boats than cars, which isn't really surprising when you learn that half the people depend on the sea for their living.

The biggest attraction of a visit to Shetland is the long hours of daylight during the summer months, it never gets very dark. You could read a book or take photographs at midnight. This is because the sun lies just below the horizon and its warm glow can be seen in the north all night long. In winter, it is dark by 3 p.m. and dawn doesn't break until about 9 a.m.

The waters off Shetland provide fish, but it is oil that is changing the face of the islands. At Sullom Voe, on the east coast, an oil-storage site has been made where millions of gallons of oil are stored. With the oil has come more jobs. The airport has been made bigger to take the extra traffic that the oil brings, and huge helicopters are a common sight in the Shetland sky where ten years ago only birds flew. Millions of sea-birds make their home in Shetland, and you would love the shaggy ponies that graze on the Islands. Although the ponies wander free, they are not really wild ponies; they belong to the crofters and they are very tame.

Twin Rabbits
Which two rabbits are identical?

Puzzle Pie

Crazy Maze
Can you help the racoon get into the empty log?

On the March
This crowd is up to no good. To slip through you'll have to step on a few toes. If you can shoulder your way to the bottom in 10 minutes, that's not bad; 8 minutes, that's good; and if you can push through in 5 minutes or less, you're liable to start a riot!

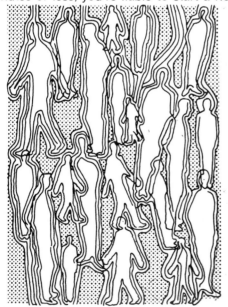

Spot the differences
Can you spot the 10 differences between these two pictures?

The Brownie Who Forgot

Helen loved her guinea-pigs. Harry was fawn with a sharp, dark face; Henry was cream-coloured and gentle.

She loved them, but she often forgot to look after them.

She didn't clean them on Monday because it was Brownie night.

She didn't clean them on Tuesday because she went swimming.

She didn't clean them on Wednesday because she went to her aunty's.

And on Thursday she forgot.

On Friday when she came in from school her mother said: "Helen, you left the door to the guinea-pigs' run half-open. You must be more careful. The next-door cat or a greedy rat might come and attack them; and, Helen, you must clean them out – tonight."

But Helen was too tired.

On Saturday morning Helen's mother said: "You must clean out those guinea-pigs today. I've told you again and again."

But Helen's friend came round

Helen loved her guinea-pigs, Harry and Henry, but forgot to look after them properly

on her bike, and Helen forgot.

On Sunday Helen's mother said: "There'll be trouble if you don't clean out those guinea-pigs. And you left the door to their run half-open again. I shall take them back to the shop if you don't take proper care of them."

When Helen came home from school on Monday she ran to the guinea-pig run on the lawn.

It was empty!

"They must be in their little house," Helen thought.

But their little house was empty too.

Then Helen remembered. "I didn't clean their run out. I forgot their fresh water. I left their little door half-open. Now Mummy must have taken them back to the shop! Oh, Henry! Oh, Harry!"

She sat down on the front doorstep and cried.

From under the hedge four little black eyes watched her. Two noses twitched.

Helen cried again, "Oh, Henry! Oh, Harry!"

A cream face and a sharp, dark face peered up through the grass. Eight creamy paws fidgeted. Two guinea-pigs came on to the lawn to nibble and skip.

Helen saw them. She jumped up. Harry ran up the lawn; Henry ran down it.

But Helen caught them and held them against her.

As she put them gently into their pen, carefully closing the door, her mother called: "Come and have your tea, Helen. It's Brownies tonight, don't forget."

When Helen came in, her mother said: "Which badge are you working for now, Helen?"

Helen blushed. "Animal Lover," she said. Then she looked up, and her expression was determined. "But I will earn it now, Mummy."

Brownies of the 5th Wigan West Pack become cowboys and Indians during a Wild West afternoon at the Wigan District "Bangers and Beans" Revels

Below: **Even if they don't win a prize, Brownies of the 1st Tisbury Pack, near Salisbury, wave flags, sing, shout and thoroughly enjoy themselves on their float in the local carnival**

E Mooney

Carnivals and Revels

Ally's Army are first-prize winners in the Shelthorpe Community Centre's Gala, Loughborough. They aren't in their uniforms, which is that of Brownies of the 12th Loughborough Pack

E Young

A Hallam

R Roberts

G Aslett

When the Mad Hatter says "all change", the guests at her "Alice in Wonderland" tea-party hastily grab plates, knives and forks and move up two places. It's great fun for the St. John's Brownies, of Ainsdale, Southport, who are guests at the eighth birthday party of the Mad Hatter (Sarah Goodwin)

Plays and

H H Timmins

The Wombles who have won a rosebowl belong to the 4th Christchurch Brownies, Dorset

Parties

A scene from the 26th Streatham Pack's Nativity play

Brownies Make Things

Picture in Frame

You will need a small box with see-through lid (the kind that sometimes holds hankies), scraps of felt, ribbons, material, coloured paper, scissors, crayons, pens or paints.

Look through your scraps of material and plan your picture. Sketch it out on rough paper first.

Now sketch it lightly inside the box. Colour the sky grey-blue and the grass green.

Cut out your characters. You could make the dog of felt, with red thread for its collar.

You could make the girl's boots of shiny black paper, and her rain hat and coat of bright silk or plastic.

Use a thin clear glue.

Colour the girl's legs and hands pink.

Draw in her umbrella with crayon or pen.

The tree may be of felt or material, or you could colour in the trunk and stick on lots of tiny paper leaves.

Lightly pencil in the shadows. You could add flowers or a bird.

Put on the see-through lid and your picture will be finished, framed and protected.

You might like to give it as an extra special birthday card.

Flower-and-Grass Pictures

You are sure to know that you can make pretty greeting-cards from pressed flowers and grasses. You can make charming and effective pictures too.

For a seascape you will need card or stiff paper, pressed grasses and flowers, glue—any clear thin paper glue will do—and crayons or water-colour paints.

On your card sketch lightly your own design. Delicately crayon or colour-wash the sea and sky. Add details with crayon or pen.

Now add the flowers and grasses. You will see sea and sky through them as if you were lying out on a cliff or headland on a summer's day.

Easter Egghead

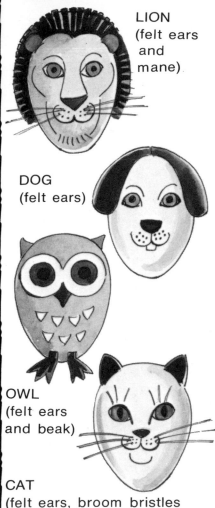

LION
(felt ears and mane)

DOG
(felt ears)

OWL
(felt ears and beak)

CAT
(felt ears, broom bristles for whiskers)

My Brownies, the 2nd Dronfield (Baptist) Pack, enjoy making Easter eggheads. Under supervision, they hard-boil eggs in water coloured with food colouring. They then decorate them, using felt-tip pens, sticky paper, scraps of felt, etc. The eggs become faces of animals, birds and people.

With scraps of felt or other material, coloured paper, etc., hats and other items can be added to the heads. Some of the eggheads we made are illustrated here. Others could be of a CLOWN, with red cheeks and mouth, blue nose, a pointed hat, and a ruffle made from a paper cake-case; a WITCH, with green eyes, green wool hair, and a pointed hat of black paper; a PIRATE, with a black patch over one eye and a cloth cap tied at the back of the head; and a CHINESE BOY, with a black wool pigtail and a yellow coolie hat.

Stood in egg-cups, the eggheads look most realistic.

A Nightie for next to nothing

Do you wear a nighty that's really in the fashion? Then convert a small man's or big boy's old shirt into one. Perhaps it has a frayed collar. Remove the collar and sew a white band round the neck.

You can shorten the sleeves —it's more fashionable to have them short for summer wear.

You'll soon have a pretty nighty.

Guide Camp Puzzle

Marilyn was a Guide who loved making up puzzles, so when Joanna, her Brownie sister, asked her to write from camp this is what she sent.

"If you want to know what our camp looks like," she wrote, "fill in this piece of paper from the directions I have written for you."

Here are the paper and directions. Can *you* find out what the camp looks like?

Draw in: A rabbit warren in the north. An oak-tree in the south-west. A gate in the north-east. The flagpole in the south. The cook's fire in the east. A marquee in the south-east. Blackberry bushes in the west. Wash cubicles in the north-west.

Marilyn added to her letter:

"If you draw a line from the centre of the gate to the foot of the flagpole you will find out which is my tent. Our Guider sleeps in the one crossed by a line from the centre of the blackberries to the near end of the marquee."

Does your finished camp look like the one on page 75?

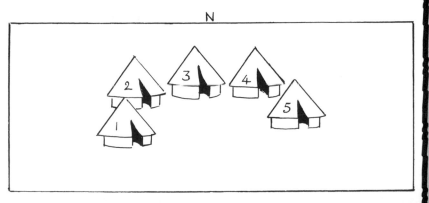

L
Ir
G
Be
a
b
M

L
S
w
ba
a
D
5t
th
ar
ba
cu
flu
is

E Morey

rownies Round e World

ide a real Red
epee a Canadian
ells Guides and
about tribal life
oms in days gone
the province of

Right: **On Pack holiday, the 26th Streatham, London, Brownies perform a delightful series of international dances, dressed in the costumes of the countries represented**
  Djatchka Kola, a dance from Jugoslavia
  Maori stick dance
  Mexican dance
  British hoop dance

panese Brownie
et ready to march
re-brigade's brass
wave their ribbons
join in Children's
brations on May
tional holiday, in
of Ueda. Fathers
ers have put up
poles from which
rdboard fish (carp)
he wind. The carp
ol of long life

H M Timmens

Step into Christmas

Get just what you wanted for Christmas—move on two places.

Not got what you wanted, but smile a Brownie Smile anyway and thank everyone nicely—take two turns.

Help mum with the washing up—take two turns.

Get the wishbone from the turkey and make a wish—move on three places.

Eat too much Christmas pudding and have to lie down afterwards—miss a turn.

You eat the chocolate bar from your stocking before breakfast (ugh!) Go back two places.

Give mum and dad their presents before you open yours—move on one place.

Hooray! It's snowing! You'll have a white Christmas after all. Move on one place.

38 | 37 | 36 | 35 | 34 | 33 | 32 | 31 | 30 | 29 | 28 | 27 | 26 | 25 | 24

39

40

41

42

43 | 44 | 45 | 46 | 47 | 48 | 49 | 50 | 51

86 | 85 | 84 | 83 | 82 | 81 | 80 | 79

87!

When you're too full of Christmas dinner to move, find yourself a dice and some friends to play with, and play our Christmas Game. It's great fun! Throw a six to start, and take an extra turn every time you throw a six again. But be careful not to throw a two. Every time you do that you have to move back two spaces! First one to reach home is the winner!

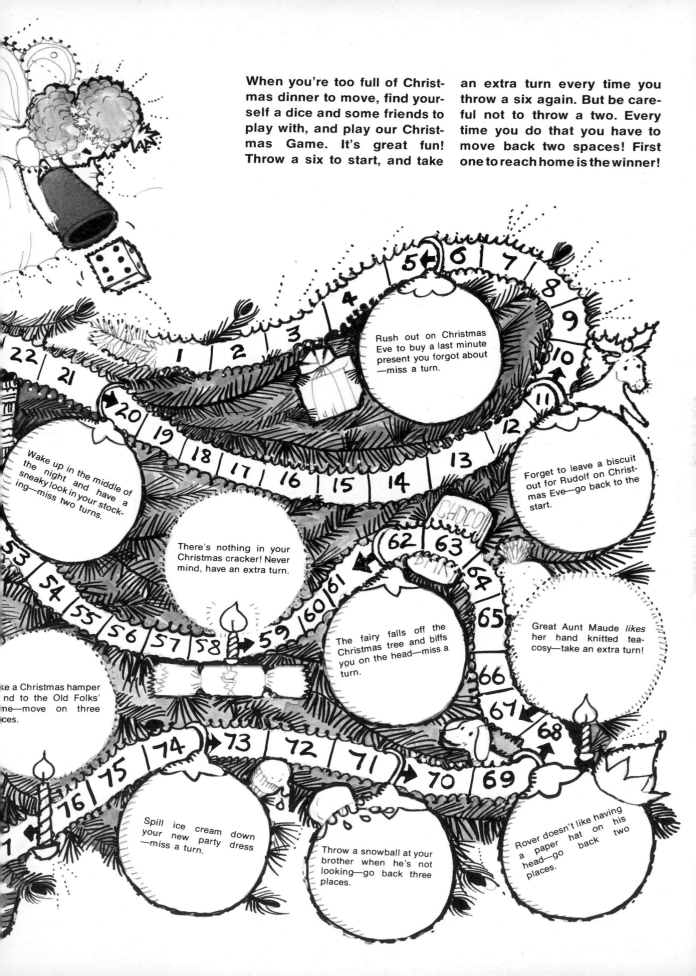

Rush out on Christmas Eve to buy a last minute present you forgot about —miss a turn.

Forget to leave a biscuit out for Rudolf on Christmas Eve—go back to the start.

Wake up in the middle of the night and have a sneaky look in your stocking—miss two turns.

There's nothing in your Christmas cracker! Never mind, have an extra turn.

Great Aunt Maude *likes* her hand knitted teacosy—take an extra turn!

The fairy falls off the Christmas tree and biffs you on the head—miss a turn.

...ke a Christmas hamper ...nd to the Old Folks' ...me—move on three ...ces.

Spill ice cream down your new party dress —miss a turn.

Throw a snowball at your brother when he's not looking—go back three places.

Rover doesn't like having a paper hat on his head—go back two places.

1 2 3 4 5 6 7 8 9 10 11 12 13 14 15 16 17 18 19 20 21 22

53 54 55 56 57 58 59 60 61 62 63 64 65 66 67 68 69 70 71 72 73 74 75 76

Random

Left: **Deborah Kendal and Louise Orchard of the 3rd Luxton Pack, Lancashire, feed a banana to a big chimp during filming of "It's a Knockout" for BBC Television**

Above: **"One good tu deserves another," said Editor of the *Brow Annual* when he hea these musical Browni play, so they oblige w another tune**

Right: **Two Brownies sha the chair-lift at a safe heig on the Guides' aerial ra way at Cowley Deer Pa Gloucestershire**

napshots

M Edwards

Right: **No, these Brownies haven't strayed into a tropical jungle. Beverly Howard and Jacqueline Cooper, out exploring with the 30th Preston St. George's Pack, find themselves among giant hogweed, two and three times taller than themselves**

Moss

Poets' Corner

THE LEPRECHAUN

I rose at dawn
And on the lawn
I found a little leprechaun.
  His face was wrinkled,
  Brown and crinkled—
    On his hammer
  Dewdrops twinkled!
      Would he stay?

      I held him tightly,
      Trembling slightly,
      Thinking lightly,
        "Mustn't let him run away."

But his stammer,
Low but clear,
Breaking through the morning air,
Fell upon my startled ear
  And made me understand.
    I must lose what I had found,
    Let him safely turn around,
    Creep back to his underground,
To Lend a Hand.

    I've been thinking now he's gone,
    Thank you, little leprechaun.

E F Drinkwater

CLUES DOWN

1. An animal with ten legs or an apple that tastes sour (4)
2. A game played on horseback with sticks and a ball (4)
3. Not bright (3)
5. Black, sticky substance used on roads (3)
7. After twelve o'clock midday (2)
9. A girl dressed in brown —like you! (7)
10. Short for Physical Training (2)
12. Fairylike creature, name of a Brownie Six (3)
13. Message of distress (3)
15. You have two, a table four (4)
16. Something with cotton on (4)

CLUES ACROSS

4. A group of Scouts (5)
6. A place where you live in tents (4)
8. The head of a monastery (5)
10. Something to push the baby in (4)
11. You call yourself this (2)
13. Short for street (2)
14. You grew these for the Gardener badge (7)
17. You could become one when you are ten (5)

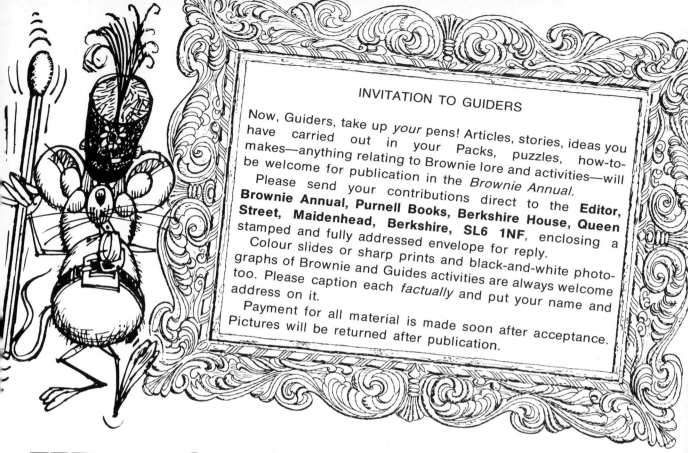

INVITATION TO GUIDERS

Now, Guiders, take up *your* pens! Articles, stories, ideas you have carried out in your Packs, puzzles, how-to-makes—anything relating to Brownie lore and activities—will be welcome for publication in the *Brownie Annual*.

Please send your contributions direct to the **Editor, Brownie Annual, Purnell Books, Berkshire House, Queen Street, Maidenhead, Berkshire, SL6 1NF**, enclosing a stamped and fully addressed envelope for reply.

Colour slides or sharp prints and black-and-white photographs of Brownie and Guides activities are always welcome too. Please caption each *factually* and put your name and address on it.

Payment for all material is made soon after acceptance. Pictures will be returned after publication.

What Good is a Brownie?

M Coverdale

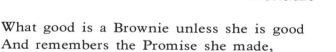

What good is a Brownie unless she is good
And remembers the Promise she made,
Who brushes her teeth and her nails as well,
Looks smart when she's out on parade?

What good is a Brownie unless she's a friend
To everyone else who's in trouble,
Who never does things by quarters and halves—
And always attempts to do double?

What good is a Brownie unless she is kind
And considers the feelings of others,
Who never is mean and always keeps clean—
And listens to sisters and brothers?

What good is a Brownie unless she is true
To her parents, her Six, and her Pack,
Who gives of her best whatever the test—
For she knows that she's on the right track?

31

This fine well-dressing, worked in flowers and other natural materials, is the creation of the 3rd Etwall Pack, Derbyshire. It was designed and made by the Pack, and with a queen bee in its centre is cleverly captioned "Born to be Queen". Well done, 3rd Etwall!

B Grimmett

It's a Challenge

Walking on tins isn't as easy as it looks, but Catherine Rule smiles as she balances

Phillippa Black tackles a sewing Challenge

It's a Challenge for Deborah Black and a Good Turn for Dad

E Rothwell

Monkey Business

The verandah of the missionary hospital in Ranaghat where I work looks out over a mango garden teeming with life—insect life, bird life, and animal life. Among the animals are monkeys. They are always interesting to watch, even though they do steal our fruit and vegetables and delight to sit up on a fence or a roof and look cheekily at us as they eat.

One day we noticed that there was much excitement and distress in the monkey world. There was such a chattering and nodding of heads, and through it all came the continuing distressed cry of a baby monkey.

After watching for a time, we understood what had happened. Out under the trees is a deep bore-hole that has not been used for some years, but has been left uncovered. Apparently a baby monkey had fallen in. As we watched, we noticed the whole tribe gather round the hole. One after another pushed forward a mother monkey and urged her with chattering, pushing and

slapping to go down the hole to rescue her little one. She would go to the edge, look down, hesitate, and then pull back; then she would go again, and again be afraid to descend. At last, urged by all her friends and relatives, down she went.

They waited and watched, but she didn't come up. What could be done? The little baby's elder brother became desperate: mother and baby down that dreadful hole and unable to come up! He ran first to one, then to another monkey in his distress, clearly urging them to do something; he pushed them forward with his little hands and he bowed his head before them, begging them to act. But what could they do? Evidently they could do nothing; they began to move back from the hole.

They could not do anything, but could we? Monkeys are not afraid of women. If we go out to drive them away when they come into the garden they show their teeth at us in a most alarming way. We decided to see whether

they would let us help. We made a rope by plaiting together three sari borders, and then we went out into the garden towards the hole. The monkeys didn't utter a sound or show their teeth. We lowered our "rope" into the hole. Mrs Monkey caught hold, and we pulled. She began to come up, but suddenly she let go and fell down again.

We tried again, and yet again, but each time the same thing happened. Then we realised that she was probably afraid of us. So we let our rope down again, and went away some distance from the hole, holding hard to the end of the rope. This worked satisfactorily, for very soon up came Mrs Monkey, with her baby clinging to her chest. As soon as she reached the top, she sprang away and ran off.

But the little brother, who had been so distressed for his mother and the baby, came forward and stood for a few moments in front of us, quiet and still, bowing his head. It was his way of saying thank you.

Clear Round

by Wendy Walker (aged 14)

The starting bell sounded
And the clapping ceased;
The stride of the big bay horse increased.
He flicked his ears
As he eyed the gate.
But he gathered himself a fraction too late.
He caught it in front,
And the whole jump swayed,
The crowd "ooh-ed" and "aah-ed"
But it somehow stayed.
They were cantering on,
The next was the wall,
And he flew it without any trouble at all.

Like an express train,
Hooves pounding,
Tail flying,
The wind in his mane.
He took off too early,
And just cleared the tape,
They were both very thankful
For this lucky escape.
She checked him a little
As they swung to the right,
And he tugged at the bit
As if wanting to fight.

They came to the double,
A little too slow,
But in the last few strides she let him go.
She pushed him on, with hands and knees,
And he flew both parts with powerful ease.
The last fence loomed,
There wasn't a sound,
She felt the power as he left the ground,
And as he landed
Applause rang round,
And the great green tannoy boomed
CLEAR ROUND.

Pony Poems

Country Rides

by **Krystyna Gajda** (aged 12)

The birds are singing, the flowers smiling,
  The sun is bursting through the sky,
My pony, Beauty is so light hearted,
  I'm sure that she would like to fly!

We trot along the country road,
  And large white pebbles mark the way;
Then when we reach the velvet grass,
  We gallop and blow our cares away.

And then we reach the highest hill,
  And see the beauty of the trees,
And lakes, and fields of golden corn,
  Gently waving in the breeze.

There's nothing like a country ride,
  To cheer your spirit and warm your heart,
And learn to love, respect and care for,
  The beautiful world of which we're part.

An essential part of our daily hack
  Is to learn and keep the country Code,
So I shut all gates, and keep my litter,
  Before we return to our own abode.

The Midnight Mare

by **Karen Fulton** (aged 12)

Motionless, a picture of beauty,
She stands,
Outlined against the sky,
And turns her majestic head,
To gaze at me.
Treading slowly,
Softly like a shadow,
She comes to me.
With tender quivering nostrils
And searching brown eyes,
Lit with mischief,
She pokes in my hand.
White ivory teeth munch,
While fleet hooves carry
Her away.
Then on her hill top,
She stands,
Black against the moon,
Before she rears,
A symbol of freedom
And beauty.

The Silver Horseshoe

Wendy had been a Brownie for three months. She was the youngest member of the Pack, but also one of the most enthusiastic. She always looked forward to Monday night, which was Brownie night. She was one of the Elves. Elves, Brown Owl told her, like to be neat and tidy, and Wendy tried to follow their example. She made her bed as neatly as she could and was careful not to leave her clothes lying about the bedroom. She always hung them up in the wardrobe or folded them up and put them in the drawers of her dressing-table.

Being a Brownie was helping her a lot, her mother said. Mummy was delighted with her tidy Brownie daughter.

One Monday evening Wendy went as usual to the church hall where the Brownie meetings were held. Everyone was there except Tawny Owl. Brown Owl explained that Tawny would not be able to come that evening, but she didn't mind, as she had something secret to tell the Brownies about Tawny.

Needless to say, the Brownies were intrigued. They loved a secret, but they couldn't think what this one was all about. They tried to guess, but Brown Owl laughed and said they must be patient for just a little while longer. She knew the Brownies would love the secret when they heard what it was.

When the time came to play games, each of the four Sixers chose one. Wendy's Six decided they would like to play "The Farmer Wants a Wife". This was Wendy's favourite game. When at last the games were ended the Brownies settled down, sitting crosslegged on the floor with Brown Owl. Brown Owl smiled at the Brownies, and when they

"What shall we buy for her?" The Brownies thought hard and made many suggestions

were all quiet said: "I don't think any of you know that Tawny Owl is getting married very soon. As she is not here this evening I thought it would be a good opportunity to tell you. I expect you would all like the Pack to give her a present."

"Oh, yes!"

"What shall we buy for her?"

The Brownies thought hard and made many suggestions. In the end it was agreed that a pretty tray would be an attractive as well as a useful present.

"Splendid!" said Brown Owl. "If you would all like to bring as much as you can next week, but not more than ten pence, we will arrange for one from each Six to go and buy a nice tray for Tawny from us all."

After this, the Brownies chattered away like magpies. This was really exciting news. Tawny Owl was to be a bride!

Brown Owl called them to order. "There is something else I want to speak to you about. When Tawny Owl and her husband leave the church, I think it would be very nice if the Pack formed a guard of honour. What do you think about that?"

All the Brownies were thrilled with this idea. They all loved Tawny Owl. It would be lovely to go to her wedding and very exciting to be a guard of honour.

"Yes—oh, yes, Brown Owl!"

One of the Elves, who was not quite sure why everyone else was so delighted, said, "Please, what is a guard of honour, Brown Owl? What do we have to do?"

Brown Owl explained. "We go into the church to see Tawny married. We sit in the pews nearest the door. When the bride and bridegroom go into the vestry to sign the register, we slip quietly out of the church and line up on each side of the path from the

church door. There are twenty-four Brownies, so that will be twelve on each side."

This was something the Brownies had never done before. The excitement was tremendous. Everyone talked at once and didn't stop until it was time for Brownie Bells.

On the following Monday evening, every Brownie gave something as her contribution to the present, and it was decided that the four Sixers should go together to choose and buy a tray.

On the Monday after that the four Sixers produced the tray they had bought. All the Brownies admired it. The handles and edging were made of wicker. On the tray there was a beautiful coloured picture of a scene from the "Swan Lake" ballet. This was covered by a glass top, so that the painting was protected. All the Brownies thought it was a present Tawny would appreciate.

But the Sixers had something else to produce. This was a little silver horseshoe

"Well done!" said Brown Owl. "We all think you have chosen a lovely tray."

But the Sixers had something else to produce. This was a little silver horseshoe.

"We saw this in the shop," explained Marion, the Kelpie Sixer, "and as we had enough money left over from the tray we bought it as a brooch for Tawny to wear and remember us by."

"She will be delighted with it," said Brown Owl, and all the Brownies agreed. "Now," went on Brown Owl, "there are two other things I want to say to you. The first is that I expect you all to come to the wedding in clean, well-pressed uniforms. The second is that one of you should present Tawny Owl with the silver horseshoe. I think, as

Wendy is the youngest Brownie, she should be the one. Do you all agree to that?"

All eyes turned to Wendy. She blushed, then a smile of delight dawned on her face. She could hardly believe she had been chosen for this honour. Every Brownie would have loved to present the silver horseshoe, but only one was angry and jealous of Wendy. She was Barbara Mundy, who was Second of the Gnomes.

"It isn't fair!" she hissed under her breath to Wendy, near whom she was placed. "You've only just joined Brownies."

"Now, Wendy," said Brown Owl, who hadn't heard Barbara, "would you like to present the silver horseshoe to Tawny?"

"Yes, I should love to," whispered Wendy.

"That is settled, then," said Brown Owl. "I will keep the horseshoe safely, Wendy, and give it to you in church."

When Brownie Bells had been sung, the Brownies broke up and chattered excitedly about Tawny Owl's wedding. They all knew the secret must not be talked about when Tawny Owl was pre-sent, so this might be their only chance!

"I don't see why you should be the one to give Tawny the silver horseshoe," complained Barbara to Wendy. "I'm a Second, and I've been in the Pack ages longer than you."

"I—I'm sorry, Barbara—" began Wendy, much troubled, but Barbara flounced angrily away without letting her finish.

Wendy's mother was excited when Wendy told her what she was going to do at Tawny's wedding. She said she would go to see Tawny married too.

The tray was presented to Tawny by Brown Owl at the last meeting before the wedding. She gave it on behalf of all the Brownie Guide Pack.

Tawny was very pleased with the tray. She thanked them all and said it would always remind her of the happy times she had enjoyed with the Brownie Pack.

The days flew by swiftly. At

A Brownie jumped forward, shot out her hand, and caught the horseshoe. It was Barbara

last the wedding day came. It was warm and sunny. Wendy was glad that the sun was shining. Brown Owl and all the Brownies arrived at the church in good time. They sat in the back pews and watched the guests come in, all beautifully dressed and looking very happy. There were white roses on the altar and vases of red carnations on either side of the chancel steps. The organist played quietly. To Wendy, the music sounded somehow sad, but she didn't know why this was so.

There was a slight stir in the porch of the church. Wendy glanced round. There stood Tawny Owl with her father, but it was a Tawny the Brownies had never seen before. In her white lace wedding gown, with a veil covering her curls, and a bouquet of white carnations and red roses in her hand, she looked beautiful. As she walked up the aisle, all the Brownies breathed, "oh!" and "ah!" in admiration.

They sang the hymns and followed the service in their prayer-books as Brown Owl had shown them. Then came the exciting moment for them to slip quietly out of the church. They lined up on each side of the path. Wendy was standing nearest to the porch of the church, holding the silver horseshoe that Brown Owl had given to her. It was a charming and dainty horseshoe. Tawny would surely be very pleased with this gift. The Brownies very patiently stood there for some few minutes in the warm sunshine; then suddenly the church bells rang out and the organ burst forth into a joyous wedding march.

Wendy was trembling with excitement. Her big moment was near. She turned her head and saw Tawny with her husband

"Thank you so much, Wendy," she whispered, and kissed her on the cheek

coming up the church towards the open door. She clutched the silver horseshoe tightly, ready to step forward when the bride appeared. Perhaps she clutched it too tightly. Somehow, unexpectedly, it shot out of her fingers, which must have acted like a kind of catapult, projecting the silver horseshoe into the air and towards the Brownies opposite. If it had hit the flagstones of the path, it would probably have broken; but it didn't. A Brownie jumped forward, shot out her hand, and caught the horseshoe. It was Barbara. Without wasting a second, Barbara thrust the horseshoe back into Wendy's hand—and in the nick of time! At that instant, the bride and

bridegroom stepped into the porch. Wendy did not wait to think about what had happened or of the disaster so narrowly averted. She gave Barbara a look of gratitude; then stepped forward and presented the silver horseshoe.

Tawny bent down and took it.

"Thank you so much, Wendy," she whispered, and kissed her on the cheek.

At that moment there was a *click*. The photographer had taken a picture of one of the happiest moments in Tawny's life—and in Wendy's.

Then the bride and bridegroom walked slowly between the rows of Brownies, Tawny smiling at each Brownie as she passed.

"Wasn't it wonderful!" breathed Ann Summers, Sixer of the Pixies, when it was all over.

The Brownies chattered nineteen to the dozen; but Wendy was more concerned about finding Barbara.

"Thank you, Barbara!" she said. "I don't know what I'd have done if you hadn't caught the horseshoe and given it back to me so quickly. I should have felt terrible if it had broken, and it would at least have been damaged if it had hit the ground. I just don't know how to thank you."

Barbara grinned. "It's all right, Wendy," she said. "I'm very glad I had a chance to make up for all the nasty things I said to you because you'd been chosen to give Tawny the horseshoe. Oh, wasn't it a lovely wedding!"

That was one thing all the Brownies were agreed upon—it had been "a lovely wedding".

Where d

You know that some birds fly away to the warm lands in autumn because our climate is too cold for them. But there are lots of small wild creatures who cannot escape from the frost and snow of winter. What happens to them?

Many of them are still about, of course, even in the coldest weather. You sometimes see their footprints in the snow. Others hibernate, making themselves as warm as possible until spring comes.

When the water in the ponds becomes too cold, it is time for frogs to hibernate. They burrow their way down into the mud at the bottom where it will always be a few degrees warmer, and stay till spring.

They Go in Winter?

What about those busy insects the ants? Where do they go? They hibernate in enormous clusters, hundreds of them curled up together in their underground nest. As they sleep, the ants on the outside get cold and wriggle their way to the middle; the others make room for them. All the time, they are very careful to see that their queen is kept in the centre of the ball, where she will not feel cold.

Squirrels only partly hibernate. They nest up among the branches of trees. Throughout autumn these little animals busily collect nuts, which they bury in the ground or in the hollows of trees. They sleep quite a lot in the winter, but they will wake up and have a meal of nuts.

Hedgehogs go to sleep curled up in a ball, and don't wake at all till the spring comes. All through the summer they eat and eat and grow really fat, for they have to last a very long time without food. Their winter nest may be in a hollow or under old tree roots or a bed of leaves.

If you have a tortoise for a pet you will know that they have to hibernate as soon as the cooler weather arrives in October. They should be placed into a box lined with straw and brought inside away from draughts and damp. Once they are unconscious it is important not to disturb them.

Most insects hibernate but usually by a different method. They survive the winter in the form of eggs, pupae and larvae, which will take on new lives as spiders, butterflies and other insects in the spring.

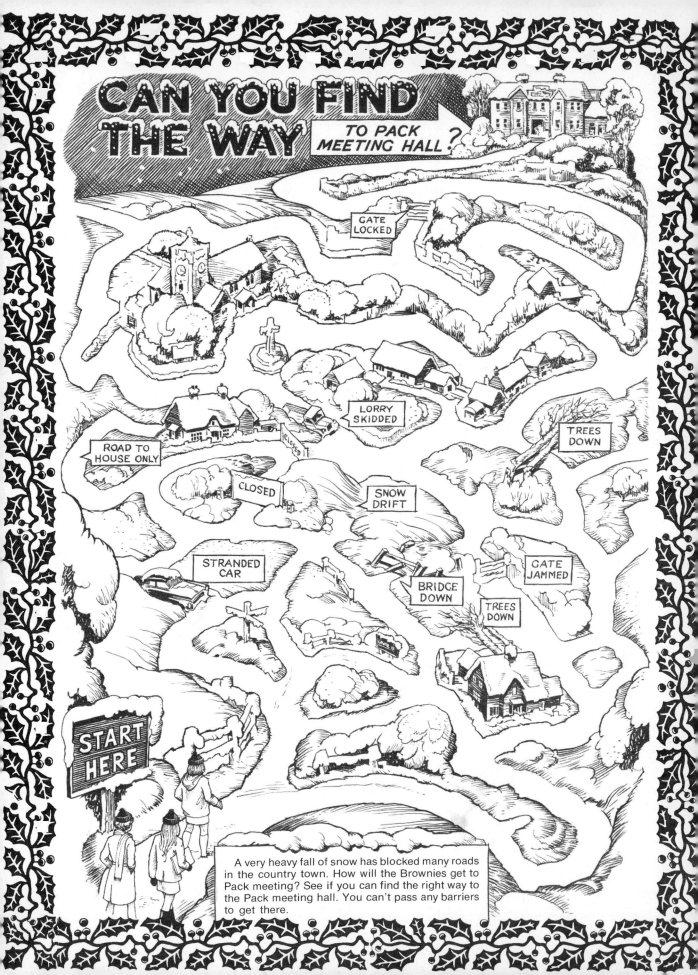

Laugh·In

Little Miss Muffet sat on a tuffet,
Eating her curds and whey,
But now she takes some crisp cornflakes
And throws the whey away!

RIDDLE-ME-REE

What kind of cat do you find in a library?
A catalogue.

What is the best thing to take when you are run down?
The number of the car that hit you.

What is the difference between a train's guard and a teacher?
One minds the train and the other trains the mind.

Why are you always tired on April Fool's Day?
Because you have just had a March of thirty-one days.

Why must a policeman be enormously strong?
Because he must be able to hold up a whole line of cars with one hand.

Why is a pig a strange animal?
Because he is killed and then cured.

What boats remind you of being punished?
Fishing smacks.

What sea-birds make you think of a train?
Puffins.

What fish makes you think of the sky at night?
Starfish.

What bird reminds you of a musician?
Sand-piper.

What is the best belt to wear on a boat?
A lifebelt.

I wish I could toss pancakes
Like Mummy, but—oh, dear!—

When I tried to toss one
On Pancake Day this year—

It came down—plop!—on Grandpa's head,
And he was very cross.

And Mummy says that pancakes need
A special kind of toss!

A Good Turn

A Play to Read and Act

CHARACTERS

Jane, *a Brownie*	Sprites
An owl (*brown and wise*)	Pixies
Leprechauns	Kelpies
Elves	Gnomes

SUGGESTIONS FOR DRESS

Jane wears her Brownie uniform.

Owl wears a long, brown, ragged-edge garment down to her ankles, with long, loose sleeves well down over her hands to serve as wings; her head and shoulders are covered with a hood, which has round eye-pieces cut out and beak sewn on.

Leprechauns wear coarse aprons over short tunics and long red stockings; they carry shoemakers' tools

Gnomes wear short, pocketed white aprons and carry brooms, mops and dusters; they are old and bent and can be bearded.

Pixies wear green aprons, with chefs' hats perched on their heads; they are perky in character.

Elves wear blue tunics and caps with ears; they have large scissors dangling at their waists.

Sprites are dressed in green and are light and airy in their movements.

Kelpies are dressed in red and wear tam-o'-shanters or berets on their heads with a feather in them.

SCENE

Jane's garden on a summer evening. Jane has just come home from Pack meeting, and is still wearing her Brownie uniform. She is sitting on a rug on the grass with a *Brownie Annual* open on her knee.

JANE: How can a Brownie do a good turn every day? What good turn could I do? *She shuts the book with a bang.* Brown Owl said we ought to help someone every day. Oh, dear, I just don't know how to begin! *She yawns and stretches.* I do feel sleepy—too tired to bother about good turns. *She curls up on the rug and shuts her eyes.*

Every Day

ENTER A BROWN OWL, WHO FLUTTERS ROUND THE SLEEPING JANE NOISE-LESSLY AND FINALLY SETTLES ON A TREE-STUMP.

OWL: Come, Leprechauns, Pixies and Elves!
    Tu-whit-tu-whoo! Bestir yourselves!
    Come, Kelpies, Sprites and Gnomes!
    Tu-whit-tu-whoo! Now leave your homes,
    And answer wise old Brown Owl's call:
    Haste to the garden, one and all!
    Tu-whit-tu-whoo!

ENTER LEPRECHAUNS, GNOMES AND ELVES FROM LEFT; SPRITES, PIXIES AND KELPIES FROM RIGHT. THEY JOIN HANDS AND DANCE THREE TIMES ROUND JANE, SINGING:

    Brownies are we of every kind,
    And we are busy folk, you'll find,
    Helping here and helping there;
    Brownies are needed everywhere
    Brownies are needed everywhere.

THEY ALL RUN OFF INTO GROUPS OF THEIR OWN SIXES AND BUSY THEM-SELVES WITH WORK. JANE STIRS AND SITS UP. SHE LOOKS ALL ROUND, IN WONDER, AT THE OWL AND THE SIXES. SHE RUBS HER EYES.

JANE: Am I still dreaming or are you an owl?

OWL: I am the wise Brown Owl from the woods,
    And these are my Brownies, busy and good;
    They have come to show you the work they do.
    Tu-whit-tu-whoo, tu-whit-tu-whoo!

JANE STANDS UP AND WALKS OVER TO THE LEPRECHAUNS, WHO ARE SITTING IN A CIRCLE, HAMMERING AND POL-ISHING.

JANE: Who are you and what are you doing?

LEPRECHAUNS *(together):* We are all Lepre-chauns, working together.

FIRST LEPRECHAUN: We've boots made of rubber, and shoes made of leather.

45

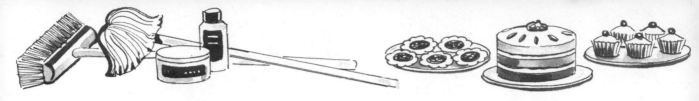

SECOND LEPRECHAUN: We mend and we polish with care and with skill.

THIRD LEPRECHAUN: We're quiet and quick and we work with a will.

JANE: (*turning away from the Leprechauns and walking towards the Elves*): That's a thing I could do—polish shoes! *TO ELVES:* You look very busy too.

ELVES (*together*); We are all as busy as Elves can be.

FIRST ELF: With needle and thread we work, you see.

SECOND ELF: To patch and darn and mend a tear.

THIRD ELF: We stitch and sew with loving care.

JANE (*turning away from the Elves and walking towards the Gnomes*): That's another thing I can do—sew on buttons and darn my socks! *TO GNOMES:* You are all working hard.

GNOMES (*together*): We are the gnomes who sweep and mop.

FIRST GNOME: We clean the house from bottom to top.

SECOND GNOME: We scrub and we rub and polish away.

THIRD GNOME: Till everywhere we look is bright and gay.

JANE (*turning away from the Gnomes and walking towards the Sprites*); I can dust and mop as well as anybody. *TO SPRITES:* Who are you busy little folk?

SPRITES (*together*); We are the Sprites and we befriend
Folks who are lonely. We're ready to lend
A helping hand wherever we go;
We like to make people feel happy, you know.

JANE (*turning away from the Sprites and walking towards the Pixies*): There must be lots of little things I can do to help lonely people. *TO PIXIES:* I see you are all working hard.

PIXIES (*together*): Pixies are we, and we like to bake.

FIRST PIXIE: Every Pixie can cook a cake.

SECOND PIXIE: We wash up too when the work is done.

THIRD PIXIE: For helping, you know, can be lots of fun.

JANE *(turning away from the Pixies and walking towards the Kelpies)*: There's always plenty of washing-up to be done in our house! *TO KELPIES:* You seem to be the busiest of all.

KELPIES *(together)*: They call us Kelpies, and we always run about,

For if an errand's to be done we're ready, there's no doubt.

FIRST KELPIE: We're very quick and nimble when we're given jobs to do.

SECOND KELPIE: But we listen to instructions, and we're very careful too.

JANE *(walking away from the Kelpies and facing front)*: I can run errands and do shopping too!

THE OWL FLUTTERS DOWN FROM HER PERCH AND OVER TO JANE.

OWL: Now, little Jane, we have shown to you
Some of the things that Brownies do,
And we're hoping now *you* have learnt the way
To do a good turn every day.
Tu-whit-tu-whoo!

JANE: Oh, yes, thank you, Brown Owl;
I know lots of things I can do now.

ALL THE SIXES RUN OUT AND CIRCLE ROUND JANE AND THE OWL, singing:
We're hoping now you have learnt the way
To do a good turn every day,
Every day, every day,
To do a good turn every day!

THEY ALL DISPERSE AGAIN INTO THEIR SIXES, AND RUN OUT THE WAY THEY CAME IN. JANE LIES DOWN ON THE RUG AND CLOSES HER EYES. THE OWL FLUTTERS ROUND HER AND OFF.

JANE *(sitting up and rubbing her eyes)*: Oh, dear, they've all gone now! *SHE LOOKS ALL ROUND.* But I remember how hard they were all working. I know now what a lot of good turns there always are to do. *SHE STANDS UP, FOLDS UP THE RUG, AND PICKS UP THE BROWNIE ANNUAL.* I must hurry indoors and do my good turn today before it's too late. *SHE CALLS:* Mummy, I'm coming in to help you get the supper ready. *SHE RUNS OFF.*

CURTAIN

Brownies Lend a Hand

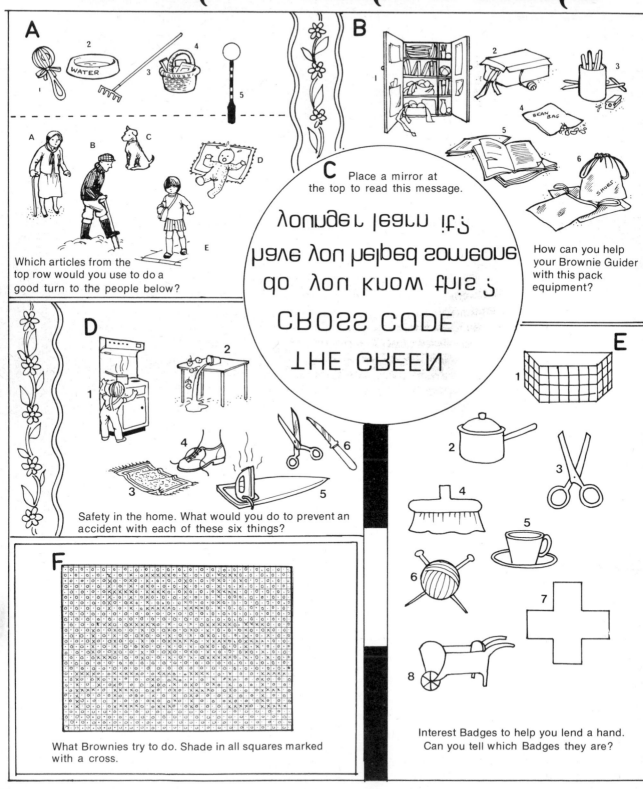

A

Which articles from the top row would you use to do a good turn to the people below?

B

How can you help your Brownie Guider with this pack equipment?

C Place a mirror at the top to read this message.

Younger learn it's
have you helped someone
do you know this?
CROSS CODE
THE GREEN

D

Safety in the home. What would you do to prevent an accident with each of these six things?

E

F

What Brownies try to do. Shade in all squares marked with a cross.

Interest Badges to help you lend a hand. Can you tell which Badges they are?

F M Brookes

Wedding bells for Snowy Owl of the 1st Moreton-in-Marsh Brownies, who turn up in force with affectionate good wishes and form a guard-of-honour

The proof of the gardening is in the growing, declare the Brownies of the 24th Selly Oak Pack, Birmingham, and hold triumphantly aloft radishes they've grown for the Gardener badge

A Freedman

Bells and Badges

H M Timmins

A pet lamb is the object of affectionate attention by three animal-lovers of the 26th Streatham Brownie Pack, London

Express Delivery Service -

seeds. How does she do it? First of all, she uses animals, and that includes you and me. Have you ever had the greeny-brown fruits of goosegrass sticking to you? Sooner or later you pick them off and get rid of them. You have delivered them to a new area! The burdock flower is something like a thistle. The hooked flower-heads may stick to the woolly coats of sheep. In some new place they will fall off or get rubbed off. The nut-like fruits drop out and burdock plants start growing in a new place. All the animals that run along the hedgerow at the side of fields, such as rabbits, shrews, hedgehogs and mice, will get some of these hooking seeds on their coats. At some time they will clean their coats, and the fruits will drop off and the seeds inside grow into new plants.

You know that squirrels collect acorns. Other trees also produce nuts that animals carry

I f we want things taken from one place to another we might post them, or arrange for them to be delivered by a van or lorry, or take them ourselves.

Nature, from time to time, wants to get seeds from one place to another. You might ask why she needs a delivery service and how does she manage one. Why can't the seeds just fall off round the parent plant and grow up round about? If they did this they would get overcrowded and not be able to find enough food in the ground, and they might find themselves completely shaded from the light by the parent plant and so wouldn't be able to grow successfully.

So, you see, Nature must arrange a delivery service for

- for Seeds!

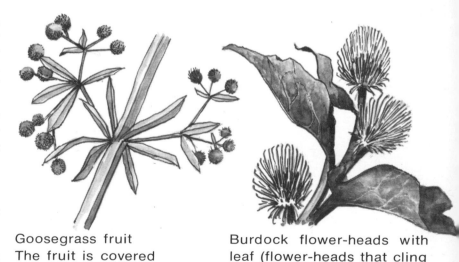

Goosegrass fruit
The fruit is covered
with tiny hooks

Burdock flower-heads with leaf (flower-heads that cling are called burrs)

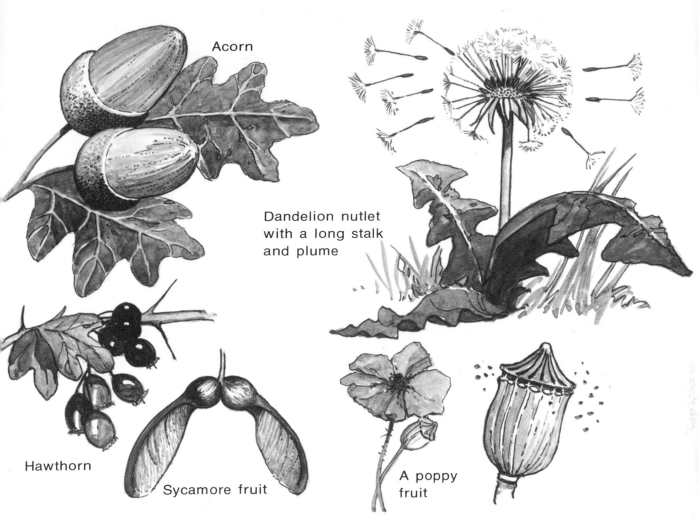

Acorn

Dandelion nutlet
with a long stalk
and plume

Hawthorn

Sycamore fruit

A poppy
fruit

away to store or eat. Many of these are either dropped or forgotten, and so the seed is delivered to a new place. Seeds inside berries, like the hawthorn, or edible fruits like cherries are also spread by animals, which eat the fruit and pass the seeds in their droppings.

Something else that carries out a seed-delivery service is the wind. Many fruits of trees have "wings", like those of a sycamore-tree. Lime, ash, and elm trees all have winged fruits, although their wings are not quite the same as those of the sycamore. Some trees and flowers may not have wings, but they do have a kind of parachute. The wind catches these tufts of hair and carries the seed along.

Think of thistledown and the dandelion. The poppy works rather differently, but the wind is still the delivery service. The poppy fruit is at the top of a long stem. When the wind swings it backwards and forwards, the seeds fly out through the holes under the lid.

Water too plays a part in the seed-delivery service. The seeds of some water-plants are carried long distances by streams or currents in the sea. There is one method that plants have, though, you may never have heard about. Some plants can shoot! No, they don't have a gun, but they do have pods. As the pods ripen, the warm sun splits them. They split open with a pop and coil upwards like a spring, shooting out the

seeds. Sit down quietly on a hot day beside a gorse-bush and you will probably hear pop, pop, pop as the pods burst and the seeds are scattered.

Keep your eyes open and try to find out which kind of seed-delivery service each plant uses.

Here's how a violet shoots out its seeds

Brownies of the 4th Christchurch Pack follow their
leader—watch their Guider
—closely as they learn to
knit

These Christchurch Brow-
nies are displaying a col-
lage they've created based
on the circus, with the one
they're holding showing a
chimps' tea-party

G Aslett

W J Beer

Peeps at Packs

"A most artistic exhibition" is the
verdict of all who come to look at
paintings, models and collages of
the 31st and 35th Portsmouth
Brownies

"Smile as you shine" is the motto of
the ten Brownies of the 35th
Portsmouth Pack who cleaned
one hundred and twenty trophies

52

M Outhwaite

Georgie Giraffe is giving the Brownies a hint that he can stoop low enough to receive any tasty titbits they may have brought along. The 7th Harrogate Hookstone Brownies are on an outing to Flamingo Land, near Pickering

E Rothwell

B Nicholson

The Brownie smile, multiplied by six—or six and a half—of the 5th Aughton Brownies, Lancashire

The cannon is loaded—with Brownies of the 3rd Hayle Pack on a visit to Pendennis Castle

53

The Mystery Next Door

Follow the Trail

A Welsh Six have laid a trail through the wood. The Elves and Kelpies are trying to find it.

Can *you* follow the trail? Here's a clue to it. The letters on the right trail spell the name of the Welsh Six.

Meet Betsy the Brownie

This is Betsy, Sixer of the Sprites. Here she is, all ready to go off to a Brownie Meeting. Can you colour in Betsy's uniform for her?

This summer Betsy went off on Pack Holiday. She wore her brown cardigan and trousers on the coach, to stop her dress becoming creased.

This is an important day for Betsy —she's going up to Guides. You'll need different coloured pencils this time. What colour do you think her tie might be?

Ready to go out to play! Betsy's bright yellow Brownie T-shirt looks good with her brown shorts.

Wallpaper beads, stamp cases, and felt boat, pincushions by the 4th Dartford (Baptist) Brownies

D Matthews

C Davey

Below: **Peg dolls by the 7th and 8th Bexleyheath West Brownies (St. Thomas More and St. Peter's Packs)**

Brownies Make Things

Icing cakes is quite a tricky job, as these Bexleyheath Brownies find as they prepare them for tea on Pack holiday

The start of the wheelbarrow race by Brownies of the 4th Winchester West Pack on Pack holiday at Crawley

Happy Holidays

Their first Pack holiday is voted the tops by Brownies of the 14th Sutton Coldfield Pack – and so is Sunday lunch!

The 20th Bromley (St. Augustine's) Brownies have toured GHQ, London, and had a good lunch, so they decide that the wildfowl in St. James's Park would appreciate one too – and they do!

Is Your Name Smith?

There was a time when people had only first names; but this was found to be very confusing, and so it became the custom for each *family* to have a name as well.

Everybody knows somebody named White, Brown, Black, Green, or Grey. How did people come to have such names? Long ago Brown was given to children as a Christian name, which is why it is the most common colour name. Sometimes, however, Brown, like other colour names, was a nickname. White-haired people might be called White and black-haired people Black; or it might be because of the colours they wore. These "colour names" are amongst the most common, but there are others that are not so easily recognised. Did you know that

think of many names that began like that. But some names are spelt in such a way that it is not clear what they were originally. For instance, a child might be named St. Clair, but when that name came to be used as a surname it was spelt Sinclair. People whose surname is Lucas are really named after St. Luke. Andrew was a very popular name for boys, but if you wanted to speak of Peter, Andrew's son, you might find it sounded more like Anderson. One name that was very popular for boys who lived in Kent was Augustine, for St. Augustine landed in Kent. But it was rather a long name for a surname, and so it was shortened to Austin. If your name is not one of those mentioned here, it would be fun to find out how it began.

My name's not Smith— it's Farquharson

My name's not Smith— it's Cholmondely

Russell means red? So do Reade, Rudd, Rouse and Rowe!

You have probably noticed that some people have surnames that are the same as Christian names, though some of them have the word "son" added. Many of these are the names of saints or are taken from names in the Bible. It was very usual to give children such names when they were christened. A boy named Thomas, whose father's name was John, would be referred to as Thomas, John's son, and in this way Johnson became a surname. You will be able to

My name's not Smith— it's Witch

Do You Know These Six Birds?

1

2. Briskly, jauntily, he walks across the lawn. He's an arrogant bird, and what an appetite he's got! Where there's food there's a starling—usually more than one!

1. He's watching for worms, and for you too, with his head on one side. See how quickly he can turn his head from side to side. He's a friendly bird

2

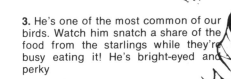

3

3. He's one of the most common of our birds. Watch him snatch a share of the food from the starlings while they're busy eating it! He's bright-eyed and perky

4. A shy little bird, one of the smallest in Britain. Look for him in hedges and bushes and on low branches of trees. The moment he spots you, up will go his tail

6. When another bird tries to get the crust he's eating, he wags his tail—not because he's pleased, but because he's angry. He's one of the loveliest songbirds of the bird world

4

5

6

5. This is the garden acrobat. Drape bacon-rind or a string of peanuts over a branch and see how he'll use claws, legs and wings to swing round and about like a trapeze artist at a circus

Baffled Birds

Can you help the birds get to the right nest by following the compass directions?

Start with the circle just above each bird.

1. **3N 1E 2N 1W 1N 2E 1N 1NW 1NE**
2. **1W 3N 2E 1N 1NW 1NE 2W 1NE 1NW**
3. **3N 1SW 2N 1SW 2E 1N 2NW 2NE 1N**

Brownies of the 5th Camberley Pack welcome two four-legged playmates, who amble up to share in their fun

Fun Days

This one didn't fall in when she swung over the stream, but two did. The 2nd and 13th Margate Packs are on a visit to a Cub Scout camp

Brownies Help at Home

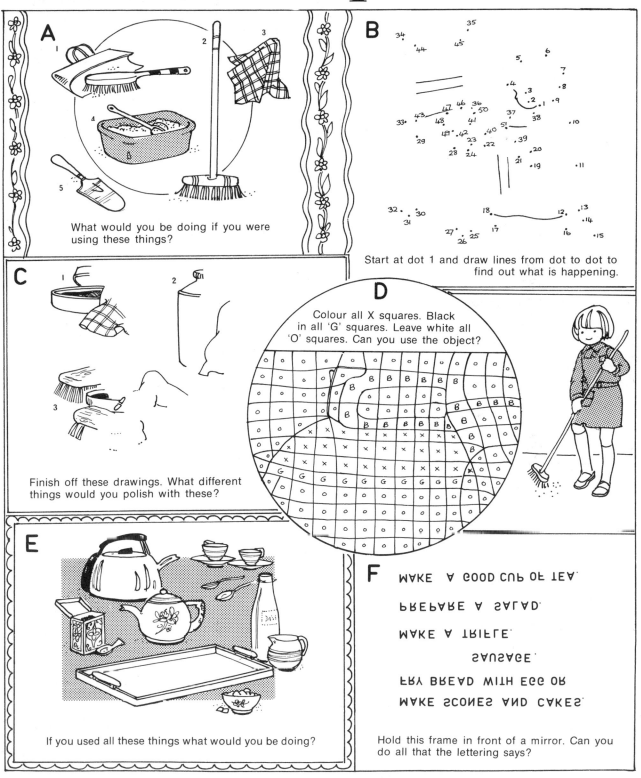

A

What would you be doing if you were using these things?

B

Start at dot 1 and draw lines from dot to dot to find out what is happening.

C

Finish off these drawings. What different things would you polish with these?

D

Colour all X squares. Black in all 'G' squares. Leave white all 'O' squares. Can you use the object?

E

If you used all these things what would you be doing?

F

MAKE A GOOD CUP OF TEA.

PREPARE A SALAD.

MAKE A TRIFLE.

SAUSAGE.

FRY BREAD WITH EGG OR

MAKE SCONES AND CAKES.

Hold this frame in front of a mirror. Can you do all that the lettering says?

The New Brownie

Jennifer James lived near Birmingham and was a member of her local Brownie Pack. She had just become a Sixer when a new Brownie arrived. Her name was Shima. You may never have heard of this name before. Well, neither had Jennifer and the rest of the Pack. They had never seen anyone quite like Shima before. Shima was an Indian girl. Her parents had just come to England. Her father had taken over a restaurant in Birmingham.

Shima could not speak English very well. This presented Jennifer with a problem, for Brown Owl put Shima in her Six. It was a real challenge for Jennifer. At her first Brownie meeting, Shima would not speak to anybody. Even Tawny Owl could not break her silence or make her smile. One Brownie forgot that Brownies are friendly and laughed at Shima's funny clothes. There were two West Indian girls in the Pack who came from Jamaica, but they wore the same clothes as the other Brownies. Shima was wearing a sari and matching silk trousers and really looked very nice. Jennifer called her Six together and remainded them that Brownies are friendly. How would they like it, she asked, if they could not speak English and wore different clothes, and were in a land among people who were a different colour and had different customs?

The Brownies listened and agreed that they should try to make Shima feel at home; but they were not sure how to go about this. They hoped that Jennifer would think of something.

Jennifer lay awake that night. She did not get to sleep until midnight. Next morning she was tired, but felt very pleased with herself, for an idea had come to her.

At the next Pack meeting Shima wasn't present, but Jennifer put forward her idea during Pow-wow.

"It's a marvellous idea," said Brown Owl, and all the Brownies agreed. "It will be our first Pack Venture," said Brown Owl, "and a most unusual one." She added that she would go and see Shima's parents and make sure that Shima came to the next Pack meeting.

The next week the Brownies were very busy and could be heard saying things like "We'll need five pounds of beef," "We'll need three pounds of rice," "You buy the spices from the market," "Could your Mum make some of her special chocolate ice-cream?" "Will this old nightie do?" and "Can we sew these together?"

What was going on? Well, Jennifer's idea was that the Brownies should have a special Indian meeting, and serve curry and rice and dress up to look like Indian girls. Brown Owl borrowed a sari from an Indian friend and painted a red spot on her forehead. There were books about other countries in the Pack's library, so the Brownies read about India and its customs.

On the evening of the Pack meeting, the Brownies arrived an hour earlier than usual. Soon the smell of curry floated on the air and rice was cooking. Presently a car pulled up outside. The Brownies hurried to the door and waited. They could hear Shima talking to her mummy.

"But me not want to go! They laugh me." The listening Brownies heard Shima's mother persuading her to go inside. The door opened, and then—Shima smiled. It was a real Brownie smile, the first one the Brownies had seen on her dusky face.

Shima saw the Brownies wearing saris and beads and bangles and Brown Owl looking like an Indian woman. As Jennifer led her to the nicely laid table, her face was radiant. "Curry!" she said happily.

If the curry was not as good as her daddy served in his restaurant, Shima loved it, and so did the Brownies.

After the meal, Brown Owl suggested that Shima should teach them an Indian song, and everybody had fun trying to learn and sing it. Best of all, even if Shima couldn't understand all that the Brownies said, she understood that she was among friends.

Now it was her turn to start learning. It took her a long time to learn the Promise, but at her Promise ceremony she was word-perfect.

"I love Brownies," she told Jennifer as she proudly displayed her Promise badge.

"And we love having you in the Pack," said Jennifer.

Orange Appeal!

Next time Mum offers you an orange, don't just eat it! Here's a super selection of ideas to show you just what can be done with an orange.

Seed Beads!

Don't throw away orange seeds —wash and dry them and then keep them until you have enough to make into a string of beads. (This will take quite a long time, so you can cheat if you want by using melon seeds as well. There should be enough seeds in one melon to make lots of jewellery!)

Once you have collected as many seeds as you need, paint them with poster paints in bright colours. You could varnish them with clear nail polish, to make them shiny, or sprinkle glitter on them while the paint is still wet, to give a sparkly effect. When the beads are quite dry, thread them together with strong cotton or fine string, to make a bracelet or necklace. Try making bangles with beads of one colour only, or using two or three colours in a pattern. Try out different effects until you find the one you like best. Knot the thread at the end, and your seed beads are ready to wear!

Clever Cloves

Long ago, noble ladies and gentlemen carried pomanders around with them everywhere. If the city street smells were unpleasant, they just sniffed their perfumed pomanders instead! Thank goodness we don't need to do that nowadays, but pomanders still make lovely presents to give at Christmas or birthdays. Hang them up in the wardrobe and all the clothes will be beautifully scented.

To make a pomander, you will need an orange with a thin skin, a piece of narrow ribbon and lots of cloves (Mum should have these in the kitchen, if not you can buy them in Supermarkets or large chemists). Tie the ribbon tightly round the orange, making a loop at the top to hang the pomander up with. Now press the cloves in firmly all over the orange, trying not to leave any gaps. Leave the orange in a warm place to dry out for a week or so, and it's ready to hang up.

Make a Mosaic

Mosaic pictures, made from tiles, were very popular as long ago as Roman times, when floors were made of mosaic tile pictures. You can make your own mosaic pictures from —guess what—orange peel!

Cut off the orange peel in fairly large pieces and spread them out on a baking tray. Leave them to dry in a warm place—an airing cupboard is ideal—for a week or more, until all the moisture has dried out of the peel. Then it is ready for use.

Now choose a background —any sort of board or stiff cardboard would be fine—and work out your design. (It's easier to do this on paper first.) A goldfish would be a good idea. Stick your orange peel design on first, then add the background—tinfoil strips for the sea, pieces of cotton wool for clouds, scraps of material for trees, etc. Now make a cardboard frame and your mosaic picture is completed!

Make Your Own Winter Flowers

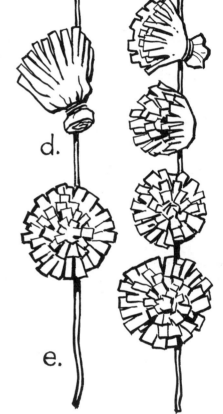

There is no better way to brighten a dark corner in any room than by putting a vase of flowers there.

But what if it is still winter and there are no flowers to pick?

Make your own!

Cut some thin, straight stalks from bushes (but ask your parents first which you should cut). Privet is very good for this purpose, and so is forsythia. They should be less than $\frac{1}{2}$-metre in length.

You now need some coloured crepe paper and some thin wire—the sort used to mend fuses is ideal, but do not take this without asking!

Cut some strips of crepe paper 3cm. wide by 6cm. long, and some more 4cm. wide by 8 cm. long.

Snip them on one of their long sides as in drawing (a).

Roll the strips as in (b) and wind wire round the unsnipped end to secure it (c).

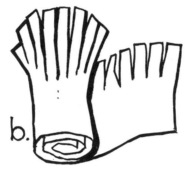

Attach the "flower" to the stalk with the other end of the wire (d).

Fluff out the snipped edges of the flower.

Attach flowers all the way up the stem, using large ones at the bottom and small ones at the top (e). Do not start too near the bottom of the stem.

Keep to the same colour for each stem.

Do you think these would look best in bright or in pale colours? Perhaps red-and-white stems or yellow ones mixed with orange would look best in *your* dark corner.

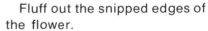

Christmas Around the World

When Christianity spread northwards into other countries many customs were adopted and the Yule Log, decorating houses with mistletoe and holly, etc., have now become traditional. The Christmas tree was introduced into England from Germany in about 1789.

Christmas celebrations have become more and more popular and throughout the English speaking world, Christmas is kept as a social holiday, and as a time for family and friends to get together.

Christmas is a time of friendship, love and goodwill, when Christian peoples all over the world gather together to celebrate the birth of Jesus.

In Britain festivities begin by sending cards, buying presents, singing carols, putting up decorations in the streets and shops and decorating the Christmas tree. On the eve of Christmas excited children all over the country hang out their stockings hoping that in the morning they will be packed with all sorts of goodies. Later, many people will go to a Christmas service at church and return with family and friends for the Christmas dinner—turkey, Christmas pudding and mince pies!

Christmas in Australia is celebrated in rather different condi-tions. December in Australia is always hot, and many Austra-lians are starting their summer holidays. Their Christmas din-ner is very much like the tradi-tional English dinner, the only difference being that the family very often gather outside to eat their meal in the sun. As dusk falls on Christmas Eve, candles are lit, and later in all the cities of Australia crowds gather to sing traditional carols.

Canada is a complete con-trast, especially in many of the scattered arctic settlements of the North, where it is dark all day at this time of the year. Here you can be sure it will be very cold and there there will be

plenty of snow. If planes have been unable to land due to bad weather conditions, Canadian Air Force pilots are ready to fly to isolated outposts where they will drop baskets of turkeys, trees and toys by parachute.

Danish country children think of their wild animals at Christmas. They put out 'Julenag', which are sheaves of grain for the birds and spread hay in the forests for deer. In the cities they will scatter crumbs of bread instead. Christmas dinner comes a little earlier in Denmark; they feast on Christmas Eve. Their meal mainly consists of porridge made with rice and roast goose stuffed with

apples and prunes and served with red cabbage and sugar-browned potatoes. Their Christmas pudding is apple cake and cream. When the meal is finished the children are allowed to see the decorated tree for the first time. The family gather to sing carols and then, just before going to bed, all the presents are opened.

The Dutch do not exchange many gifts at Christmas although the children put out shoes under the chimney on December 5th. This is the birthday of St. Nicholas, the Good Bishop of Myra, who loved giving presents. According to Dutch tradition it is on the night

of December 5th that St. Nicholas—Sinta Klaas—rides on his white horse, stopping to fill the good children's shoes with presents. But any naughty children will have their shoes taken away!

In the town of Bethlehem, the birthplace of Jesus, pilgrims gather at dusk on Christmas Eve to sing carols. Later, a procession makes its way to Manger Square. Here on the very site where Jesus was born the bells ring out at midnight and a choir sings 'Gloria in Excelsis Deo'. Over the altar of the church of the Nativity a bright star shines, just as it did nearly two thousand years ago.

Brownie Badge Sewing Cards

Make these four outlines into Brownie badges of other lands and hang them up in your Six corner or in the Pack hall. All you need to do is trace the outline of each badge on to thin card, make holes where shown, and thread wool along the outlines. When they see the finished badges all the Brownies in your Pack will want to make some.

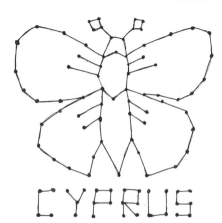

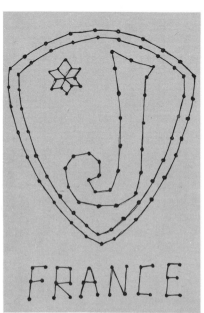

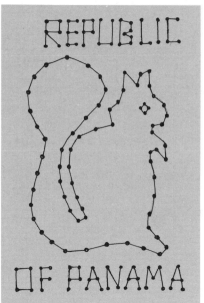

Belgium: badge gold; letters gold and brown.
France: badge navy blue; green J; pale blue star; letters gold and brown.

BLIC

NAMA

Be a Busy Brownie

Twenty-five ways to fill a wet afternoon

1. Fill empty milk bottles with different levels of water and hit the tops gently with a fork.

2. Add up the numbers of your birth date eg. 3/5/1971=26=8—to find your lucky number!

3. Stand on your head and work out how to get right way up again.

4. Have a cheese and jam sandwich. Sounds nasty, but tastes nice!

5. Make your own birthday cards from pieces of material, feathers, glitter, etc. stuck onto card—or even small sweets!

6. Balance a pencil on your nose. If you can't manage it across your nose, maybe you could do it lengthwise.

7. Make an animal bookmark from felt. Add long floppy ears which will show you where you open the book!

8. Edible jewellery? Paint little pasta shells and stick them onto velvet to make pretty bracelets or necklaces!

9. Go through your old copies of 'The Brownie' and make a scrapbook of your favourite articles. Give it to a friend who's ill.

10. Make up a secret code and write yourself a letter in it. A week later, try to decode it.

11. Eat a slice of bread buttered on the wrong side!

12. Draw a picture without once raising your pen from the paper.

13. "Adopt" a ladybird and give it a name. Can you find out what ladybirds like to eat?

14. Try to dress all in one colour. You might have to dress up as something silly to be able to do it!

15. Crush up some rose petals and put in a bowl with a few cloves. Pot pourri smells lovely.

16. Catch a falling leaf and make a wish.

17. Make up your own fairy tale, with you as the princess.

18. Ask mummy if you can paint the outside of your goldfish bowl—your goldfish will be pleased to have a change of scenery!

19. Or make curtains for your budgie's cage!

20. Stick some shoeboxes together and cover with wallpaper to make a doll's house—or a set of little shelves for ornaments.

21. Plant some orange seeds in a bowl of earth. This time next year you could be eating the results.

22. Make a miniature garden—arrange some moss and tiny plants on a tray, with a little mirror for a pool.

23. Take one double-page spread of a newspaper, concertina—fold it across, and draw the shape of a person on it, with the arms stretching right out to the other edge.
Cut round the figures (through all the thicknesses of paper). Open it out and you'll have a chain of dancing ladies, which you can colour in.

24. Start collecting used stamps, silver paper, etc. All sorts of charities would be grateful for your "rubbish". Your Brownie Guider will have the addresses of charities.

25. Wish everyone you meet a Happy un-birthday—with a big Brownie Smile!

POTATO CUT PRINTING

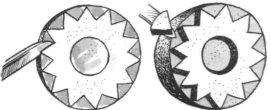

Using three colours, make a pattern and print it by any method you like. Think carefully about your design and the colours that you are going to use before you start to print. The following example is an ideal way to do some printing.

Use a nice, firm round potato cut in half. With a small penknife cut on the lines to a ½ cm depth

With the point of your knife cut out the bits from the side. Be very careful always to cut away from yourself

Here are two more designs. Use simple shapes. You can make any designs you think you can cut cleanly. You can print in bright colours, using powder paint with not too much water. Paint evenly on to the potato with a good big brush

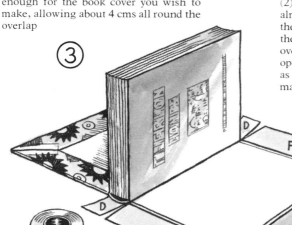

You can use your different designs like this. Use a good piece of paper large enough for the book cover you wish to make, allowing about 4 cms all round the overlap

(1) Place the book with the covers open as shown; in the centre of the paper fold over at (A) only

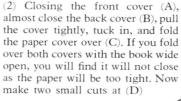

(2) Closing the front cover (A), almost close the back cover (B), pull the cover tightly, tuck in, and fold the paper cover over (C). If you fold over both covers with the book wide open, you will find it will not close as the paper will be too tight. Now make two small cuts at (D)

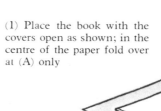

Fold the ends (F) over first, then the sides (G). (3) Open out and cut the overlaps to the right size up to the corners (E); taper the ends of the two side pieces. Insert and stick down neatly with transparent sticky tape. The small piece (D) can be tucked inside the binding

When preparing your potato for printing, it is advisable not to leave it too long before it is used, otherwise the potato can become very soft and your printing will not be as precise as it might have been when the potato was freshly cut

Answers

"Hasn't anybody seen my tube of glue . . . ?"

THINKING DAY PUZZLE (p. 10)

1A—Smile, 2D—Inches, 3D—Flowers, 4A—Write, 5D—Friends, 6D—Birthday, 7D—Round, 8D—Robin, 9D—Turn, 10D—Toothbrush, 11A—Branch, 12D—Roads, 13D—Prayers, 14D—Margaret, 15D—Mother, 16D—Teacher, 17A—Imps, 17D—Ironing, 18A—Owl, 19D—Lad, 20A—Good, 21D—Badges, 21A—Ball, 22D—Lying, 23A—Song, 24D—Models, 25D—Message, 26A—Eyes, 27D—Left, 28D—Venture

PUZZLE PIE (p. 18)

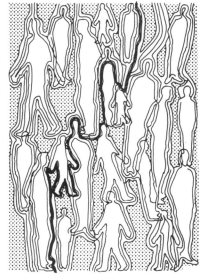

Rabbit: 2 and 8 are the same

TOADSTOOL CROSSWORD (p. 30)

Down: 1—crab, 2—polo, 3—dim, 5—tar, 7—pm, 9—Brownie, 10—PT, 13—SOS, 15—legs, 16—reel. *Across:* 4—Troop, 6—camp, 8—abbot, 10—pram, 11—me, 13—st, 14—flowers, 17—Guide

GUIDE CAMP PUZZLE (p. 23)

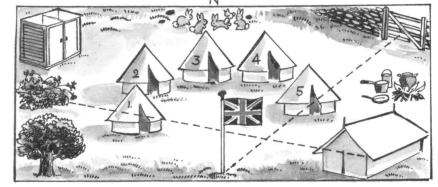

BROWNIES LEND A HAND (p. 48)

A1 and D2 and C3 and B4 and A5 and E. B1—repair beanbag, 2—wash bags, 3—sharpen pencils, 4—repair equipment boxes, 5—repair, clean and recover Pack books, 6—tidy pack cupboards. D1—turn pot handle away, 2—wipe up liquid, 3—turn down rug, 4—tie child's shoelace, 5—switch off iron, 6—put knife and scissors in a safe place. E1—Safety in the Home, 2—Cook, 3—Needleworker, 4—House Orderly, 5—Hostess, 6—Knitter, 7—First Aider, 8—Gardener.

FOLLOW THE TRAIL (pp. 56, 57)

The trail spells BWBACHOD, a Welsh Six

BAFFLED BIRDS (p. 63)

1—C, 2—A, 3—C (either 1 or 3 must be a cuckoo)

BROWNIES KEEP FIT (p. 76)

B1—ball, 2—ropes, 3—hoop, 4—skates. C—Skip fancy steps, leapfrog, climb a pole, swim 15 yards, roller-skate. D—Apple, toothbrush, carrot, toothpaste, water. E—Run, skip, jump, hop, dance, swim, walk, sleep, laugh. F1—Swimmer, 2—Agility, 3—Skater, 4—Athlete, 5—Dancer, 6—Gardener, 7—Pony Rider, 8—Cyclist.

BROWNIES HELP AT HOME (p. 65)

A1—brushing up dust, 2—sweeping, 3—dusting, 4—washing up, 5—gardening. B—girl dusting chair. C1—polishing furniture, 2—polishing brass or silver, 3—polishing shoes. D—an iron. E—set a tray and make a pot of tea. F—make a good cup of tea; how to prepare a salad; make a trifle; fry bread with egg or sausage; make scones or cakes.

BIRD CHORUS (p. 63)

1—robin, 2—starling, 3—sparrow, 4—wren, 5—bluetit, 6—blackbird

Brownies Keep Fit

A

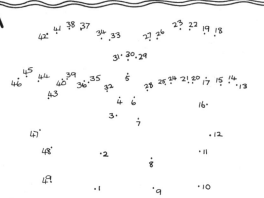

Start at 1. Draw a line from dot to dot to find something to wash often.

B

Write down the letters in each group. Rearrange them to find four things to use to keep you fit.

C

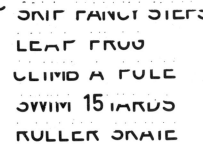

SKIP FANCY STEPS

LEAP FROG

CLIMB A POLE

SWIM 15 YARDS

ROLLER SKATE

Finish off the top half of these letters. Can you do these activities?

D

How many things can you find that help to keep your teeth strong?

E

Start at R. Miss every other letter to spell out things to do to keep fit.

F

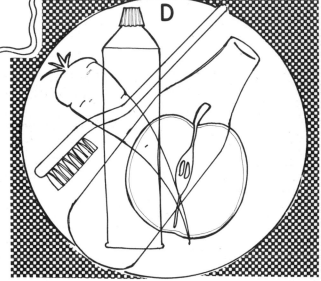

1 2 3 4 5 6 7 8

Symbols from Interest Badges. You must be fit to do them. What are they?

Funny Photos

Here, and overleaf, are some amusing animal photographs which we have collected. Which one is your favourite?